SCOTLAND

An Imprint of Scholastic Library Publishing
Danbury, Connecticut

Published for Grolier
an imprint of Scholastic Library Publishing
Old Sherman Turnpike, Danbury, Connecticut 06816
by Marshall Cavendish Editions
an imprint of Marshall Cavendish International
1 New Industrial Road, Singapore 536196

Set ISBN: 0-7172-5788-6
Volume ISBN: 0-7172-5800-9

Library of Congress Cataloging-in-Publication Data
Scotland.
p. cm.—(Fiesta!)
Summary: Discusses the festivals and holidays of Scotland and how the songs, food,
and traditions associated with these celebrations reflect the culture of the people.
1. Festivals—Scotland—Juvenile literature. 2. Scotland—Social life and customs—Juvenile literature.
[1. Festivals—Scotland. 2. Holidays—Scotland. 3. Scotland—Social life and customs.]
I. Grolier (Firm). II. Fiesta! (Danbury, Conn.)
GT4845.A2S36 2004
394.26411—dc21   2003044850

For this volume
Author: Julie Ross
Editor: Yeo Puay Khoon
Designer: Benson Tan
Production: Nor Sidah Haron
Craft and Recipes produced by Stephen Russell

Printed by Everbest Printing Co. Ltd

Adult supervision advised for all crafts and recipes,
particularly those involving sharp instruments and heat.

CONTENTS

SCOTLAND

Scotland is situated to the north of England. Two-thirds of the country is mountain and moorland. One of the most beautiful regions of Scotland is the Highlands – which is home to the hardy "Highland Cow." The landscape is rugged with many "lochs," or lakes in Gaelic, and the ancient language of Gaelic is still spoken by some people.

◀ In the Highlands today many people still wear the traditional kilt (and in other parts of Scotland too!). The kilt is worn by men in Scotland and is made of **tartan**. In Scottish history the pattern of the kilt and the color depended on which "clan" the men were from — it helped tell who was an enemy and who was a friend in battles.

▼ **Edinburgh** is the capital of Scotland. It has an ancient castle built on top of an extinct volcano in the center of the city and is a very big tourist attraction to many foreign visitors.

▲ **Haggis** is a very famous Scottish dish made from mashed sheep's intestines. When haggis is served, it is accompanied by someone wearing a tartan kilt and playing the bagpipes.

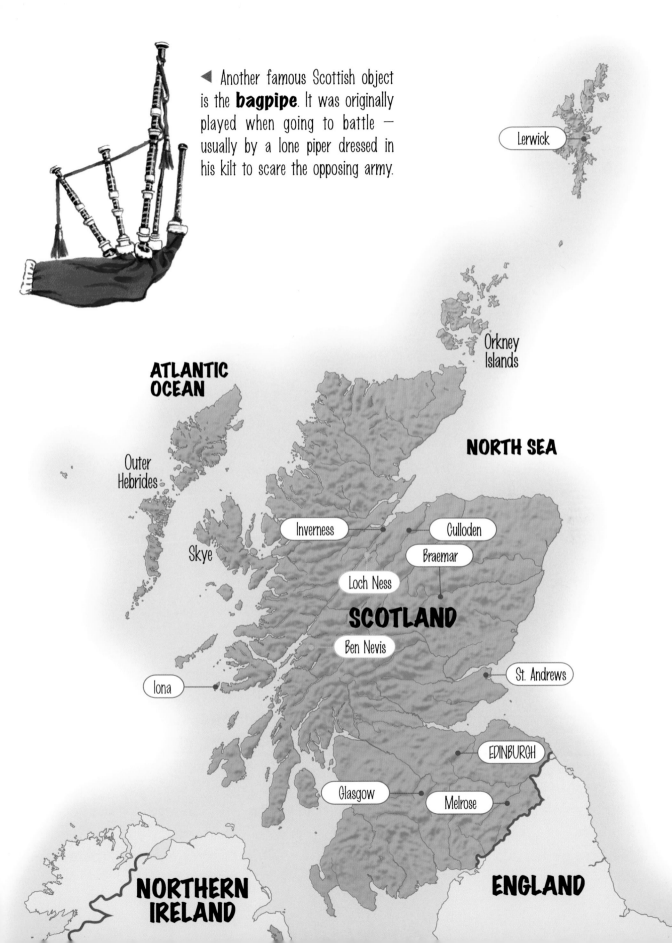

◀ Another famous Scottish object is the **bagpipe**. It was originally played when going to battle — usually by a lone piper dressed in his kilt to scare the opposing army.

Lerwick

ATLANTIC OCEAN

Orkney Islands

NORTH SEA

Outer Hebrides

Skye

Inverness

Culloden

Braemar

Loch Ness

SCOTLAND

Ben Nevis

St. Andrews

Iona

EDINBURGH

Glasgow

Melrose

NORTHERN IRELAND

ENGLAND

RELIGIONS

Today two-thirds of the Scottish population belong to the Church of Scotland (or Presbyterian church). There are also Roman Catholics, Free Presbyterians, Methodists, and Protestants.

THE EARLIEST PEOPLE to live in what is now known as Scotland arrived more than six thousand years ago from England, Ireland, and Europe, where they hunted with stone tools and lived off the land and sea. Europe's "Beaker People" arrived next, bringing with them bronze and weapons, while the Celts brought iron.

The Romans tried to conquer Scotland. However, they failed, and "Hadrian's Wall" was built to keep the Picts in Scotland from attacking further. It was built around A.D. 121, and remains of the wall still exist today. The Picts were a Scottish tribe known for their tattoed bodies and beautiful carvings on large stones, which you can still see in parts of Scotland today.

Christianity arrived in Scotland through St. Ninian, a traveling bishop who established a religious center in Galloway, where he died in A.D. 397. For many centuries his tomb remained a place of pilgrimage.

This is a crucifix worn by Christians in Scotland.

With the Scots, a Celtic tribe from Northern Ireland that settled in the west of Scotland in the fifth century, came St. Columba ("Dove of the Church"), who founded a religious center on the Island of Iona, which still exists today. His mission was to convert the Picts and other tribes in Scotland to Christianity, thereby taming them. Iona quickly became the headquarters of the Celtic church and was an important center of Christianity despite the retreat of many of its monks to Ireland during the Viking invasions. It was during this time that the cathedral was destroyed, but it was rebuilt again in 1072, 1506, and 1900. The rule of St. Columba and the remaining Celtic church were also destroyed at this time. It is surely true to say that religion has played a big part in Scottish history.

Many Celtic influences are still found in Scotland today, through Scottish folk music and Celtic craft. Gaelic, the language of the Celts, is still spoken in the Highlands.

GREETINGS FROM **SCOTLAND!**

The ancient language of Gaelic, which is a traditional Celtic language introduced to Scotland around 400 B.C., was spoken in all of Scotland until the twelfth or thirteenth century. Today the language still exists and is spoken mainly by people in the Highlands and Islands. Although the language is in decline, efforts to revive Gaelic are being made. Numerous Gaelic words still linger in everyday speech, which makes the Scottish form of English quite difficult to understand.

How do you say...

How are you?
Ciamar a tha sibh?

I am fine
Tha mi gu math

Goodbye
Mar sin leibh
Oh Yes Och Aye

Thank you
Tapadh leat

I'm sorry
Tha mi duilich

Good morning
Madainn mhath

SAINT ANDREW'S DAY

St. Andrew's Day is marked on November 30 every year in Scotland as a reminder of Christianity coming to Scotland.

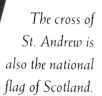

The cross of St. Andrew is also the national flag of Scotland.

Andrew and his brother Peter were two of the original apostles. However, very little is known about Andrew except that he was a fisherman from Galilee who spread the Christian religion in Greece and Asia Minor. It is believed that he was crucified on a diagonal cross by the Romans in Greece.

Three hundred years later the bones of Andrew were to be moved as far away from Greece as possible by the Roman Emperor Constantine. Legend has it that a Greek monk was warned of this by an angel in a dream and intentionally moved the holy relics to Scotland – more specifically to St. Andrews, where a chapel was built to house them and, later, a cathedral. At this point Scotland was believed to be the "end of the Earth."

St. Andrews became the religious capital of Scotland and a destination for many pilgrims until the Scottish reformation. During that period the followers of John Calvin, who was a French religious reformer, wanted to get rid of all traces of Catholicism, so the relics were removed from the cathedral. Today a plaque marks the site of his bones in the ruins of the cathedral at St. Andrews.

St. Andrew used to be a fisherman before he became an apostle and helped spread Christianity.

According to legend, an angel appeared and told a Greek monk to move the bones of St. Andrew to a safe place.

In 832 Andrew became Scotland's patron saint. According to legend, an army of Scots was facing an English army, and the Scottish king prayed to St. Andrew for help. When he saw the cross flag of St. Andrew (the saint had been martyred on a diagonal cross) against the clear blue sky, the Scottish king swore that if the Scots won the battle, St. Andrew would live forever as the patron saint of Scotland. The Scots won that battle, and since then the cross of St. Andrew has been the national flag of Scotland.

9

LOCH NESS MONSTER

Loch Ness is situated near Inverness, in the north of Scotland.
It is a freshwater loch, or lake, of which there are many in Scotland.

WHAT COULD BE MORE Scottish than "Nessie"? Does she or doesn't she exist?

Loch Ness is deep and dark, and provides a fabulous hiding place for the Loch Ness Monster – or Nessie, as she is fondly known. She has appeared in many cartoons, songs, and Scottish folklore – although she is known to be quite shy, especially when there are cameras around. But she is also believed to be quite friendly and curious.

There have been many sightings of Nessie in and around the loch – some dating back as far as the sixth century, when St. Columba wrote in his diary about seeing a serpent. Photographic evidence, though, has only been around since the 1930s. They were the first recorded sightings, but many of these images are blurred due to mist.

The Loch Ness Monster has been described as having a very long neck, with many bows. The estimated length of the creature is about forty feet.

Perhaps the most convincing evidence to date is a sighting in 1954 by a fishing boat from Peterhead, when a recording of "a large object" was made at a depth of around 480 feet to 100 feet above the bottom of the loch. There have also been many other convincing sightings of the creature, and there is a large amount of evidence to suggest that Nessie does exist – although she still remains a mystery to many! Many people still visit the loch today, hoping to catch a glimpse of Nessie. There were more sightings of her recently, and Nessie was once again spotted and described as having a long black neck and being bowed in shape. But once again, she became camera-shy!

MAKE YOUR OWN CELTIC KNOT

YOU WILL NEED

Graph paper
Pencil
Color markers
Eraser

1 Mark off a section of graph paper 2 units high and 12 units wide. (We have taken one unit as 4 small squares on the graph paper.) Put a dot at the one-quarter and three-quarter point along the vertical center line of each unit square. (Do all these steps very lightly in pencil.)

2 Draw diagonal lines at 45 degrees to connect the dots on opposite sides of the rectangle.

3 Extend every other set of diagonal lines to form points above and below the initial lines. It is important that you extend the diagonals as shown, not the ones in between.

4 Connect the points with arches. Note that the arches that move into corners end with points. Also, make sure that your arches are of the same width.

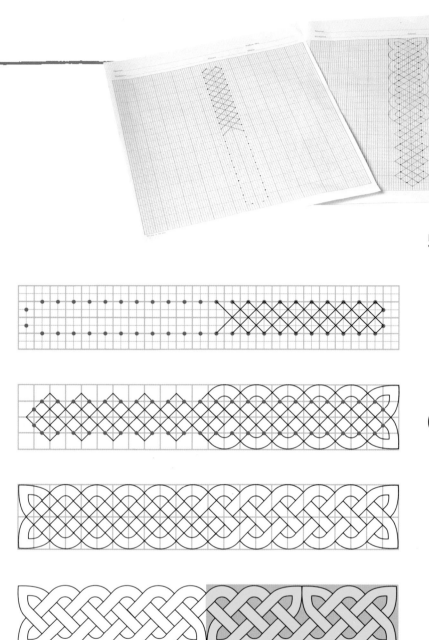

5 Erase the dots. Erase one cord's lines from each intersection to create the illusion that one cord goes over the other. Remember that you must alternate between "overs" and "unders" to achieve the weaving effect.

6 Clean up any stray marks. This stage is known as the knotwork plait. Break the plait at appropriate intersections by erasing the lines where they cross. Then reattach the lines so that each cord goes back on itself instead of continuing along the plait. Fill in the cords with the color of your choice and the background with a dark or neutral color.

13

HOGMANAY

"Hogmanay" is one of the most celebrated events in Scottish history, when people all over Scotland celebrate in a very carefree and happy way.

Nobody is really sure where the "Hogmanay" name came from, but it is widely believed that it came from the Gaelic *"oge maidne,"* meaning "new morning."

During this event large celebrations take place all over the country. There are street parties, playing of bagpipes, lively music, traditional Scottish dancing, and lots of whisky for all adult partygoers. Songs that date back to various parts of Scottish history accompany lively dancing, which reflect victory celebrations after a battle.

Traditionally, torchlight processions, fireball swinging, and the lighting of New Year's fires were practiced. Today these traditions are still carried on in many remote parts of the country and are always accompanied by lots of "whisky toasting to new beginnings."

The celebrations begin in the early evening and finally climax at midnight, with the sounds of clock bells, bangs, and ships' sirens to bring in the New Year. This is always followed by lots of kissing of everyone around and linking arms to the sound of "Auld Lang Syne" – "out with the old... and in with the

Scotland is the largest producer of whisky in the world. It is well known for its finest malt blends of whisky that are as old as 25 years. There is always whisky at any Scottish celebration, but not for the children.

Good-quality barley that is high in starch is malted and made into whisky with water and yeast.

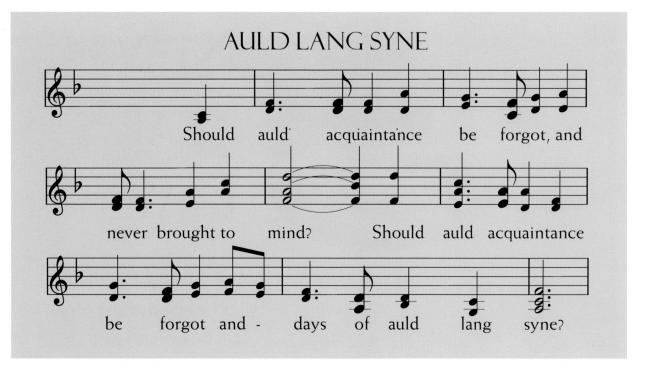

AULD LANG SYNE

Should auld acquaintance be forgot, and never brought to mind? Should auld acquaintance be forgot and-days of auld lang syne?

new" can be heard by participants celebrating the New Year, who are hoping for better things in the New Year.

In all the customs of "Hogmanay" it is firmly believed that the New Year must begin on a very happy note. Bad luck from the previous year is left behind, and there will be abundant good luck in the New Year.

"First footing" comes right after midnight, when people leave their own homes to visit family and friends, armed with a present. Traditionally, the present is a lump of coal for the fire. In return a dram of whisky is given to the visitor. It is good luck to be the first to arrive after midnight, since the next year will be a good one for the family receiving the first visitor. According to the legend, this visitor should be a tall, dark stranger and not blonde. The fear of blonde visitors came about because of the Viking invasions between the eighth and twelfth centuries.

In Scotland today Hogmanay is celebrated on a very large scale in the big cities and also in the countryside, where people travel miles to attend and take part in the hours of celebrations, with parties carrying on for days!

For good luck Scots offer a lump of coal to their family and friends during "First footing."

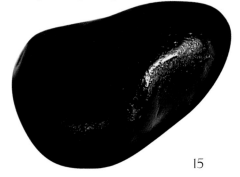

NEW YEAR'S DAY

Pure butter shortbread has long been a traditional treat over the festive season.

As part of the New Year celebrations, the tradition of "first footing" continues into the first day of the new year, when family and friends visit each other.

Friends and family sit down for a large feast. They also drink whisky and eat lots of food, such as oatcakes, soup, cheese, potatoes, turnips, haggis, shortbread, and anything else that is traditionally Scottish. This feasting still takes place in both the cities and the countryside.

Quite often this is the one time in the year when families really get together to catch up on the events of the past year. That is because many families live in different parts of Scotland and they don't travel often to visit each other. It's a great opportunity for children to meet up with their relatives. It's also a time for the adults to reflect on the last year and to bring everyone up to date. When the adults meet, they make "New Year's resolutions," in which they decide on things that they want to do differently in the new year. For example, it might be to "visit each

Cheese is served as part of the traditional feast to celebrate the new year.

16

1 Mix oatmeal, baking soda, and salt together in a bowl. Add the melted fat and hot water. Stir well until it makes a soft paste.

2 Sprinkle some oatmeal on a board. Form the dough into a round shape, and roll it out thinly, adding oatmeal to the surface if necessary to prevent sticking. Cut off excess oatmeal.

3 Set the oven to 375 degrees. Heat a griddle or heavy frying pan.

4 To test the correct heat of the griddle, sprinkle it with a little flour. If the flour browns at once, it is too hot; it should take a few seconds to turn color. Bake dough on the hot griddle until the edges begin to curl. Turn over, and cook the other side. Do not let the oatcakes brown; they should be a pale fawn color.

5 To oven bake; place on a large ungreased baking sheet. Bake for 15-20 minutes.

6 Put oatcakes on a wire rack to cool. They are delicious served with cheese.

OATCAKES

SERVES SIX

8 oz fine (pinhead) oatmeal
$\frac{1}{2}$ tsp of baking soda
Pinch of salt
2 tbsp of bacon fat or melted butter
1 $\frac{1}{4}$ cup of hot water
Extra oatmeal for rolling

other more often." If these resolutions are said in front of a group of people, then the person will be expected to try to make them happen through the coming year.

There will also be parties in the evening.

There is singing and dancing once again, with live bands performing at public functions and traditional bagpipe music in the home. Again, this can last up to a few days, especially in the rural communities.

Soup forms part of the traditional New Year's spread.

BURNS SUPPER

Robert Burns is Scotland's most-loved poet, and Burns Suppers have been held in his honor for over two hundred years. It is perhaps the other most celebrated event in Scotland and by Scots around the world.

Dry oatmeal is used to make traditional haggis; it gives the haggis a crunchy texture.

After addressing the haggis, a toast of whisky is raised to thank the haggis during Burns Supper.

Robert Burns is Scotland's most renowned poet. He was born in Ayrshire on January 25, 1759. He came from a poor family but was very interested in English and literature.

His first brush with fame occurred in 1787, when a large volume of his poetry was published, and he managed to buy a farm in Dumfriesshire that he ran unsuccessfully for three years. After that he slumped into a period of drudgery believing that his poetry had no value, and he died in his thirty-seventh year in Dumfries.

Perhaps Robert Burns' most well-known work is "Auld Lang Syne," which is sung around the world at the stroke of midnight on New Year's Eve.

Robert Burns appeals to many people today because he stood for the average man on the street and is celebrated with a "supper" every year. This doesn't just happen in Scotland but around the world too! This "supper" consists of quite a strict list of events and always takes place in the evening.

First, who has ever heard of anyone thanking

a piece of food? Robert Burns toasted the famous Scottish haggis, which is a traditional Scottish dish of minced sheep insides, spices, and oatmeal wrapped in a sheep's stomach. At the "supper" it is brought in on a platter accompanied by a man playing the bagpipes.

The toast begins like this: "Fair fa' yer honest, sonsie face, Great Chieftain o' the Puddin' race!"

When the haggis has been "thanked," it is then stabbed with a knife, and the feast begins. The haggis is eaten together with neeps and tatties, or turnips and potatoes, and Scottish whisky. The turnips and potatoes have been boiled separately in large pots and mashed. The texture of the turnip and potatoes goes very well with the haggis since they are smooth, while the haggis has a slightly crunchy texture.

For this occasion the men wear tartan kilts, while the women usually wear tartan sashes.

TATTIE-AN'-NEEPS

This is usually served together with haggis.

YOU WILL NEED
1 lb potatoes, peeled
1 tbsp of chives or shallots, chopped
1 lb turnips, peeled
1 tbsp of heated butter or fat
Salt and pepper

1 Boil the vegetables separately.

2 Drain the vegetables.

3 Mash well together, adding salt, pepper, and butter or fat.

4 Season to taste, and serve very hot.

EASTER

In Scotland, as in other Christian countries, Easter is celebrated by many attending church services on Good Friday and Easter Sunday.

Church services take place all over Scotland on Good Friday, which families attend in order to recognize the crucifixion of Jesus, the Son of God. This is normally quite a solemn affair.

Christians believe that Jesus arose from the dead on Easter Sunday to prove that he was the Son of God, and it is more of a celebration.

Many children look forward to this day of fun. They get to paint eggs using different colors and designs.

This is all done the night before, using paint or food dye. Egg-painting competitions also take place in which prizes are awarded for the best-decorated egg.

When the eggs have been painted, families head out to their favorite hill slope to meet many other families that have

gathered. The day is spent rolling the eggs down the hill slope in a competition. The egg that reaches the bottom of the slope unbroken wins a prize. It is a very happy day, when everyone joins in and has fun – usually bringing picnics with them if the weather is good. Picnickers lay out blankets and enjoy the day sitting on the grass.

In the morning it is believed that the Easter bunny will bring an egg to children. It is usually a large chocolate egg, and children are allowed to start eating it right away, even before they venture out for their day of "egg rolling!"

The symbolism of the egg is very important on this day since it is seen as a new beginning or a new start in life – bringing hope to many people.

Fun-filled Easter bunny hunts are organized for children, and those who can find them are rewarded with an Easter egg each.

People pack picnic baskets full of goodies and celebrate Easter by enjoying a picnic and egg-rolling competitions when the weather is good.

Chocolate eggs of different colors are shared among children to celebrate Easter because eggs symbolize a new start in life.

BONNIE PRINCE CHARLIE

One of the most famous stories in Scottish history tells how the Scots met the English in battle. It is about a very brave man called "Bonnie Prince Charlie."

ALSO KNOWN AS the Young Pretender, Bonnie Prince Charlie led his supporters in an uprising against the English in 1746 at the Battle of Culloden. He was the son of James Edward Stuart, a Catholic and son of the exiled English king, James VII, who fought very hard for Scotland's independence. James Edward Stuart was also known as "the Old Pretender." He fled to France in 1719 after failing to regain his throne.

His son, Bonnie Prince Charlie, came back to Scotland to try to recapture the throne in 1745 with the support of the Highlanders. This was known as the Jacobite rebellion but was only supported by the Highlanders.

Many lives were lost that day at Culloden. The Highland army was badly defeated by the Duke of Cumberland's army, and there was much bloodshed. From that time the English banned the formation of private armies and slaughtered many Highlanders who had nothing to do with the rebellion.

Scottish Highland history from then onward changed dramatically, since a whole way of life was lost forever.

Bonnie Prince Charlie was hailed as a hero in the Highlands. After five months of evading capture, he finally escaped to France. In 1750 Charlie secretly visited London. He tried for years to reclaim his right to the throne but could not get enough support. In 1788 he died, after having lived his life in exile.

HIGHLAND GAMES

People from all over the world come to Scotland to attend the Highland Games, which have been around for the last hundred years.

"The Highland Fling" is a dance based on the antics of a stag on the hillside, with the grouped fingers and raised arms representing the antlers.

Traditionally, the Highland Games are held once a year, normally during the summer period, with the most famous games being held at Braemar.

It is a big gathering where hundreds of Scots compete in traditional events. Tartan can be found everywhere, in kilts worn by both men and women and even on rugs for picnics. Every year Queen Elizabeth attends the games.

Competitions that take place include Highland dancing, in which boys and girls compete in dances such as "the Highland Fling." This is a traditional solo dance that is believed to mimic the stag and became a wild dance of victory.

A series of bagpipe bands from all over Scotland come to take part in the festivities too – wearing all types of tartan kilts with many colors.

Tartan dates back to the Roman times, but it became associated with the clan system after the seventeenth century. Clans were set up as families related by blood. Each clan wore a specific tartan depending on the family name. Tartan comes in different patterns and colors, and traditionally can only be worn by a

Men and women taking part in "the Stone Put" event have to try and throw a heavy, round stone as far as possible.

member of the family who bears that name.

The bagpipe is very Scottish. It is believed to have been introduced either by the Romans or the Irish. It is also associated with battles since it was and still is used by Scottish soldiers. When Scots around the world hear the sad sound of bagpipes, they generally become very homesick, since it reminds them of the various battles for independence.

Strong men compete in the Highland Games events to show off their strength. In "Tossing the

There are many different tartan designs in Scotland, each one belonging to a different clan.

Caber" a very long piece of wood that looks like a telephone pole is first rested on a man's shoulder. When he runs forward, he flips the pole over, so that it falls forward in front of him. The man who can toss the heaviest and longest pole wins.

Then there is "the Stone Put," which is like a shot put except that a

During the Highland Games people pack black buns for a picnic. Black buns derive their name from their dark color and are actually fruitcake.

stone is thrown instead. The round stone weighs seventeen pounds for men and eleven pounds for women, and only one leg can be moved when throwing the stone.

In other countries like America and Australia, Highland gatherings have become very popular. Many Scots immigrated to these countries during the Highland Clearances of the late 1700s, and they can now proudly celebrate their Scottish roots.

THE EDINBURGH MILITARY TATTOO

The Edinburgh Festival, of which the Military Tattoo is a part, began in 1947 after the Second World War to boost the culture of Scotland.

The Edinburgh Festival is now one of the most famous festivals in the world, attracting some of the best artists and performers globally. The festival lasts for three weeks in August every year and has grown dramatically in size, with a fringe festival happening before the start of the official festival program.

During the festival Edinburgh comes alive for twenty-four hours a day. Plays are staged, exhibitions are held, and jugglers and performers line the streets. People everywhere marvel at the scenes of joy and creativity. An enormous fireworks display is always held at the Edinburgh Castle cliffs at the end of each festival. It is an explosion of color and noise, and people throng to the best spots to try to get a glimpse of the fireworks. The city of Edinburgh comes to a standstill every year when the closing ceremony takes place.

A military tattoo is held every year as part of the festival at Edinburgh Castle. The word "tattoo" comes from the closing

Cannons are fired to signal the start of the impressive display of military regiments that is the Edinburgh Military Tattoo.

Even horses join in and form part of the cavalry display in the military parade.

time cry from the inns of the Low Countries, *"Doe den tap toe,"* which means "turn off the taps." The Edinburgh Military Tattoo is a celebration of many traditional Scottish Regiments and their military skills. Other regiments from different countries also take part in this military display, which people flock to see from all over the world. It is an amazing sight, including guns, horses, cavalry, cannons, pipe bands, and finally the lone piper with the haunting sound of his bagpipes.

Edinburgh Castle is a stunning site for the Military Tattoo, which has been held there since its beginning. It is a romantic and beautiful castle – located in the Old Town of Edinburgh.

Street performers juggle balls to entertain festival-goers and create a carnival atmosphere.

SKYE BOAT SONG

Speed bonnie boat, like a bird on the wing

Onward, the sail - ors cry

Ca - rry the lad that's born to be king,

O - ver the sea to Skye.

MAKE A VIKING HELMET

YOU WILL NEED
Thin cardboard
5 paper fasteners
Tin foil
Paper glue

1 Cut a strip of cardboard about 20–22 inches long and 1 inch wide. Make the band fit around your head by wearing the strip around your head, and then fix the size of the band with a paper fastener.

2 Cut a second strip of cardboard about 18 inches long and 1 inch wide.

6 Spray the helmet with silver spray paint, and allow it to dry.

7 Apply glue on the inside of the strips of the helmet but not on the nose guard.

8 Cut a rectangular sheet of tin foil, and attach on the inside of the helmet, sticking the tin foil to the strips. Trim excess tin foil with a pair of scissors.

3 Punch a hole in one end of the strip, and attach it at the rear of the headband. Insert a paper fastener to attach.

4 Put the band around your head, and place the second strip over your head (from the back to the front), leaving the longer end to hang down over your nose to create a nose guard. Mark this spot with a pencil, and remove from your head. Punch a second hole, and insert a paper fastener.

5 Cut a third strip of card about 16 inches long and 1 inch wide. Place the helmet on your head, then hold one end of the strip on the side of your head, and put it over your head until it reaches the other side. Mark each spot with a pencil. Remove helmet, and punch two holes at the spots. Attach to the helmet with paper fasteners.

UP-HELLY-AA

The Viking invasion and settlement from the eighth to twelfth centuries had a big impact on the Scottish people on the northern islands of Scotland – namely, Orkney and Shetland.

The Vikings sailed from Norway in graceful longboats with beautifully carved dragon heads upfront. They invaded countries all over northern Europe.

They were a very fierce race, well known for razing entire villages. But they were also very skillful at making jewelry. They made very nice brooches and bracelets out of silver, which was valued more than gold by the Vikings. They also made beads from amber, since it was believed to have healing powers.

"Up-Helly-Aa" was introduced to Shetland on the twenty-fourth day after Christmas about one hundred and fifty years ago. The festival consists of a procession through the main street of Lerwick. It first began as a group of men shouting, firing guns, beating drums, and blowing horns. Later on it became a festival of lighted torches. In the procession a longboat is dragged through the streets and finally set on fire in the dark of night, lighting up the skies. The festival is very noisy, and people who participate certainly know how to celebrate well, since it lasts into the wee hours of the next morning!

As the grand finale to the celebrations, people carry torches (above) through the streets and set the Viking longboat alight.

The Vikings believed that amber had special healing powers, so they valued it highly and used it to make jewelry.

WORDS TO KNOW

Cavalry: Troops trained to fight on horseback.

Crucifixion: The death of Jesus on the cross.

Dram: A small drink of liquor.

Drudgery: Tedious, menial, or unpleasant work.

Exile: The condition of being forced to live outside one's country.

Flint: A very hard, fine-grained quartz that sparks when struck against steel.

Gaelic: The language of the Gaels, especially of the Highlanders of Scotland. It is a branch of Celtic.

Haggis: A traditional Scottish dish consisting of the minced insides of a sheep mixed with spices and oatmeal, and boiled in sheep's stomach.

Infamous: Having an exceedingly bad reputation.

Longboat: A type of Viking ship.

Martyred: Put to death for devotion to one's religious beliefs.

Pilgrimage: A religious journey to a holy place.

Resolutions: Formal expressions of intentions.

Saint: Title of a person given in the Christian Church — especially the Roman Catholic Church.

Solemn: Deeply earnest and serious.

Stag: Male deer with antlers or horns.

Symbolism: The practice of investing things with special meaning or character.

Toast: A form of thanks and celebration accompanied by a speech and the raising of a drinking glass to a person or an object.

Vikings: The seafaring people from Norway who raided the coasts of northern and western Europe from the eighth through the twelfth century.

ACKNOWLEDGMENTS

WITH THANKS TO:
Neda Namazie, Katharine Brown, Senthamarai Rogawansamy, Lynelle Seow, and Anita Teo for the loan of artifacts.

PHOTOGRAPHS BY:
International Photobank (cover), Sam Yeo (p. 6, p. 8, p. 9, p. 15, p. 17 bottom, p. 20, p. 24 top, p. 25 top, p. 26 bottom), Yu Hui Ying (all other pictures).

ILLUSTRATIONS BY:
Enrico Sallustio (p. 1, pp. 4-5, p. 7) and Lee Kowling (p. 11, p. 23).

SET CONTENTS